Deliriums

Azadeh Atri

Deliriums

Acknowledgements

I am forever indebted to my mother, Nahid Atri,
who ignited in me a love of literature and poetry.

Special appreciation and sincere gratitude to Anna Booth,
who read the first drafts and encouraged me to
send my Deliriums to a publisher.

I am grateful to Stephen Matthews
who provided the opportunity for my voice to be heard.

Deliriums
ISBN 978 1 76041 646 1
Copyright © text Azadeh Atri 2018
Cover artwork: Azadeh Atri

First published 2018 by
GINNINDERRA PRESS
PO Box 3461 Port Adelaide 5015
www.ginninderrapress.com.au

Contents

War, migration, survival, agony, regret, unspeakable pain…   7
The Tree I Loved and the Mysterious Man   29
Matures   44
Love and Death   55
Fragments   59

For Mum, Dad, and Yegi
and
in loving memory of
Farman, Mary, Mutti and Kambiz
whose true friendship is greatly missed

War, migration, survival, agony, regret, unspeakable pain, and perhaps never-healing wounds

It was your birthday yesterday. There hasn't been a birthday that I have missed. Any! Even after you died. Do I miss you? Yes, heaps. Every day. After all, you were a friend that I never had and so far, it seems, I will never have.

Remember the day you told me that I'm like a daughter that you never had? Then you said, 'No, not a daughter, because it doesn't show the deep connection and friendship beyond the parental instinct. Parents love their kids unconditionally, as if they have to love them, they have to feel the deep connection. Parents are meant to love their kids. You are my soulmate, my friend, the friend that I never had, despite all these people around me.'

I told you it was likewise. But harsh as it might sound, I prefer you dead. Why? Because you were in such pain that there was no cure, no remedy. No one could help, not even your soulmate, the friend that you never had. It's kind of very ironic, isn't it? Love was not enough. Deep understanding was not enough. That sublime and extraordinary friendship was not enough.

I guess I'm old enough now to understand why. Sometimes it takes more than love to be able to survive. Who knows what I'll be thinking when I'm older. Maybe in twenty years' time, in some Rumi-like ways, I will believe in love and its power to overcome all obstacles once again.

Or maybe, in some Khayyam-like ways, I will finally agree with you and start drinking and drinking while stargazing and being amazed at the immense universe, being enchanted by the endless and infinite ways of existence. Maybe! But for now, I don't think love is the answer to our miseries and definitely not to yours.

Nothing was enough to compensate for all the agony and pain you were in, let alone soothing it. The soulmate was not enough, nor the love of all those many students of yours who looked up to you. I'm still angry that I couldn't help, we couldn't help, that my love, our love, was not enough.

I wish you were never born into that family, that country. I wish you were never born at that time. I wish you were born in the distant future somewhere in France or Switzerland, somewhere on a different planet. That would suit you better.

Did you ever have fun at all? I guess I'll never know. At least you had all that money to spend on anything you desired. My memory is faint but you had about four houses. You had about five pianos, and two digital keyboards that you rarely touched. You had that gorgeous red Jeep that I loved to climb on its roof. The irony is that you didn't even drive. You hated driving and you got other people to drive you around.

But you loved technology. That I know. It was the only thing which could still fascinate you. You had the first computers, the first digital cameras, the first mobile phones, the first of everything from the world of technology, the first spy cameras, the first spy pens. And for sure you had fun with all those.

I think having the spy camera was out of necessity. You noticed one of your students was going to the forbidden room and stealing some of your money on a regular basis, almost every week when she was supposed to wait for her lesson in another room, behind another door, the door to your teaching studio.

The forbidden room was a name we invented ourselves. It was simply a large area which included your very dusty and messy office, with lots of cigarette butts and the alluring smell of tobacco that you used for your pipe, and two bedrooms.

Your whole apartment was a bit mysterious with all those creased hessians on the doors, walls and the ceiling. Well, I have to admit that it didn't look just a bit mysterious. It could actually freak many people out. Only the floors skipped having creased hessians. What a genius idea for soundproofing your place. Every picture, every painting was mounted on that coarse fabric. It was there that I noticed hessians have a special smell. I grew up with your hessians, so I never thought they were scary or strange. In fact, hessians hold a special place in my heart and my handicrafts. Just recently, I made two gorgeous curtains out of this unique fabric and embellished it with some delicate laces. My hessian look very feminine; everyone asks me where I bought it.

As a child, I found your design different but very exciting. I just wanted it to be brighter. That's all. In fact, I was quite entertained by the enigmatic feel of the whole place and I loved taking toffees from the crocodile-shaped ceramic bowl. The crocodile looked happy and kind, and I loved the way it naughtily stared at me every time I reached for a coffee-flavoured toffee.

As a grown-up, I still hold the same views about your place. It was very Harry Potterish. I told you many times that if only Madam Rowling knew you had created these fascinating and incredible rooms way before she had imagined her scenes. She could perhaps be a good friend of yours, a friend who shared that bit of your imagination. I wish she could meet you. You needed someone like Marquez with his magical surrealism, or Gunter Grass with his bitter yet enchanting imagination.

Anyway, the entire place had dimming lights, with thousands of books, music scores, CDs, old gramophone discs, artistic objects and above all the smell of tobacco mixed with your Davidoff Cool Water, which permeated everywhere.

I can understand why everyone wanted to see what you had in the forbidden room, behind the forbidden door. It was the only door no one was allowed to open and look through. This added to the mystery of the entire space. It was as if you staged your whole house to fit and match the dramatic life you ran.

You were the director, producer and the sole performer of your enigmatic play. Many of us simply loved this eccentricity; some even worshipped it. For some, you were formidable. Many others were daunted. They couldn't go past beyond the staging; they were not quirky enough to appreciate it, let alone understanding your creative mind. Their haunted eyes revealed it all. And this became a subject of our jokes: faces of huge question marks, faces of huge exclamation marks.

The waiting room had long been impregnated with all sorts of stories people made in their heads about this mysterious place while waiting for their lessons or for their children's lessons. God knows what kind of inspirations they took from the place.

The waiting room felt heavy somehow. You could sense a bizarre and curious energy. It was saturated with years and years of the innermost thoughts of so many people. The invisible weight of all those floating thoughts. Heavy-weighted ones were floating closer to the floor and the light-weighted thoughts were jammed under the ceiling ready to squeeze out. The smell, the light, the silence of the room intertwined with the faint sound of someone's good or bad playing from the other side of the door, the weight of countless untold stories. You left no other option but encouraging your visitors to think and think, imagine and imagine. That was your greatest talent of all.

After all these years, I still wonder whether the waiting room with its peculiar energy pushed that girl into the forbidden room. Or was it the weight of her own untold story plus others that threw her to the other side? I still wonder to this day. She could no longer control herself, the imagination and temptation got so real, so powerful and so wild that only snatching some bits of the other side could quell her feverish weekly cravings.

Your staged waiting room aroused all sorts of emotions in that girl but the one she surrendered herself to was evil, was like black magic. You were suspicious about her for a long time. You just needed proof, and the spy camera was the perfect answer to your curiosity. You didn't care about the money at all. You had more than enough. You were more amused by the entire situation than upset or angry. You had a great deal of fun looking for the right spy camera and where to place it in the forbidden room.

You extremely enjoyed every second of being a detective for that short while. After all, being behind cameras was your greatest hobby. You videoed and recorded all of our performances in the Dark Age, the time you decided you would never ever play again, the time that had no returns, no turning backs, the time that dragged you in like a vortex, the time that we watched you drowning deeper and deeper in slow motion, that swampy time.

Watching students performing through the lenses of your high-tech cameras became your number one enjoyment and obsession. You had the best sound recording devices. But none of your professional cameras suited the situation. You needed to spy quietly on a student who not only dared to step into the forbidden room but also betrayed your trust. You hated dishonest people, yet you hoped she was stealing some of your marvellous books.

You set the camera at an angle that captured her entrance to the room from above. It was also zoomed in on a clock next to the door. So her invasion to the room could be documented accurately, second by second. The most chilling documentary I have ever watched in my life: the silence; the strange eyes of the girl when she stepped in quietly and looked around; the clock, which brutally showed the hour, the minutes, the seconds; the hessian walls; the messy desk with all those cigarette butts and your drinks, one for cleansing and one for intoxicating.

It could have been a Hitchcock scene. She went through all your desk drawers, looked at the computer, found the money in the envelope that you intentionally put among your papers. Your masterful baiting trapped her in no time. She took it all. She looked at the clock checking the time; it was time to go; she disappeared in a blink of an eye. Can't remember her face or her skin colour or her hairstyle. I think she had long hair. All I can remember is the look in her eyes, that triumphant and satisfied look. That demoniac sense of achievement was terrifying.

The camera kept recording after she left the room. The silence and the clock became even more daunting and unbearable after she left. It was like Dali's clocks in that bare land of *The Persistence of Memory*. It was truly haunting. The most suffocating few minutes I have ever watched.

Again, the way you staged your plot was genius. It was like one of Visconti's scenes in *Conversation Piece*. I'm not saying it was the same, I'm saying it felt the same. Well, you knew what you wanted out of that scene. After all, you had the most extraordinary collection of movies by well-known directors. You were always a man behind the camera, like those directors. Only if you were born in the distant future.

She was in her late twenties, born to a very wealthy family, married to another very wealthy man. She wasn't poor, she wasn't a druggie. She was just bored. She did not need the money at all. Her stealing was a psychological condition, the same condition which was once acted by Juliette Binoche in *Bee Season*.

You confronted her; She denied. You showed her your bone-chilling documentary; she cried, she begged for secrecy, for mercy, for forgiveness. You forgave her right away but wanted her to seek help from a psychologist in return for confidentiality. You asked her not to ever be back; she cried, she apologised a million times, she vanished with shame. You wished she were a book thief.

And then came your magic spy pen. I was perhaps the first victim of your new amusement. We shared the same sense of humour and I was also fascinated by any spy gadgets you had, so you knew I would love your latest buy and I wouldn't mind your funny little game.

You gave me the pen to mark the orchestral reduction of Tchaikovsky's first piano concerto when I was discussing it with another student of yours whom I had a crush on at the time. You had guessed my infatuation with that guy. That poor, poor guy! You knew me too well. I never discussed the first stages of being infatuated with someone else, unless I was a hundred per cent sure about my feelings and blah blah...

Anyway, I had accepted to play the accompaniment part with him and we were talking about the first few pages of the grand majestic concerto. The pen recorded whatever we chatted about. Thank God the conversation never went beyond that marvellous music, that marvellous being Tchaikovsky. I was not worried about myself. You knew I would tell you everything anyway; everything, including details of every crush I had on any guy. I was just worried about that poor guy.

After a couple of hours, you showed up in the room and wanted your pen back, then you mischievously played the recorded conversation.

I burst into laughter and said, 'Thank God it was all about uncle Tchaiko.'

I don't remember whether the poor guy laughed or not. I hope he did. Perhaps he didn't, because I still remember his puzzled look. Also, we never ended up performing the concerto together.

Years later, when I was learning the third movement myself, his look was still so fresh in my memory. I couldn't help myself thinking how vicious we were that day: you with your vicious project, me with my vicious laughter, and us with our vicious sense of humour. I hope he has forgiven us both. The concerto is so tightly woven to that day, to that pen, to that infatuation of mine. I have never listened to it the same as the day before that day.

To be fair, at least one thing went all right in your life. It could have been worse. You could have been that destitute musician who everyone pitied. Well, you worked your arse off so as not to be that very poor piano teacher. Twelve hours of teaching to forget your sadness. It was not emotionally rewarding but was financially at least.

The lucky ones, the chosen ones or the talented ones could see the genius side of you as a musician, as a human being, the side that showed your deep and sensitive understanding of the world, of the arts and music.

The year you died, I drowned myself in teaching. I had to. It was so dark. It was so bitter. Worked six days a week, taught at least eight hours a day. By the end of the year, I had accumulated a lot of money. I injured my vocal chords too. It was due to over-talking, over-teaching, and over-everything.

The irony is that unconsciously I did something you used to do all those years to overcome your unspeakable pain. But I couldn't do it beyond that ominous year. I still wonder how on earth you could bear all those hours of teaching for so many gloomy years. Maybe you didn't care at all, maybe that's why you had to drink so badly, or maybe you only spent your energy on the chosen ones, who weren't that many anyway. Maybe you were a true workaholic besides being a true believer in that alchemic liquid.

I know I'm brutally honest about this and I know you wouldn't mind. After all, we openly discussed this a zillion times over my sour-cherry tarts and a thousand cups of black tea that I had while you tried to cleanse with a thousand cups of thyme and lemon tea.

We had our good share of fights and fiery, furious arguments. You were perhaps the only person who liked and even admired my brutal honesty. That's why I was the friend you never had. You said I had no pity and I couldn't be fooled by others' self-pitying. You said I could see through all that.

You were always looking for that pure honesty and I was always ready to pour out all my uncensored thoughts and opinions. Pure honesty hurts everyone. At least I haven't met anyone who is not offended or emotionally hurt by that. They pretend they are not. Oh man! *But they are so badly hurt.* Their eyes are so revealing, they sell them out.

It seems no one is strong enough to take it in; no one respects honesty. You have no choice but playing the game of politics, the game of diplomacy, the game of words. But we communicated with our naked minds, naked words, no covering, no embellishment, no pity. As if we knew there was no time for any game, we preferred to be bare, to be transparent. I never had a drink with you and you were always pissed off about it, because everyone else had, and besides, you knew how much I loved my vodka and how much I could drink with my other friends.

You knew I would never ever drink with a person who obsessively saluted the most celebrated chemical endeavour of Zakaria Al-Razi. You knew everything about me. Everything. You knew about those that I fell in love with, those I couldn't stand at all. You were my wise confidant. You knew it all. Even those things that I never said out loud but you could read in my eyes. After all, that is what soulmates do.

You knew that I could read your eyes too. I called you one morning. You sounded so sick, so distressed. I rushed to your place. It took me an hour. Traffic was crazy; it always was. Your first student was coming in four hours.

You were in the forbidden room. There was white powder everywhere, on the desk, on the floor, on the wall mirror, on your books, on your shirt, in your symbolic drinks, the cleansing and the intoxicating ones. The room was stuffy and darker than usual. I could hardly breathe. You were frantically powdering your face. It was all over your eyebrows, ears, nose, and even lips. You were so feverish, so lost, so out of this world.

I asked, 'What the hell are you doing?'

You said, 'I have to cover it, I can't bear it.'

I asked, 'You want to cover your face or is it something else you want to cover, or perhaps you're not covering, but revealing it all?'

You said all of that. The redness was killing you. You wanted a white face like old days. You said it was what the make-up artist used to do when preparing you for live performances on the TV before the Dark Age.

I said, 'I'm sure she didn't powder your lips, nostrils and eyebrows like this.'

You said, 'It's not white enough.'

I hugged you, tried to calm you down. You immediately reminded me of the drunken character in *The Little Prince*. He drank to forget he was a drunk. With you, even drinking was not soothing. You could still see the red face behind the drunken mind. Even the powder had lost its whiteness. You couldn't be fooled even as a drunk. You saw too much.

I said, 'I thought you hated make-up and those who put it on.' Wasn't it what you liked about me, not wearing make-up and facing my pure bare face everyday?

None of those people we talked about was ugly; none needed to cover their face. They just lacked something. They felt they would never ever be enough without that thick or thin touch of magic. They were running away from their own beautiful faces. Their beauty was so overwhelming that they had to cover it up, had to convert it, had to fake it. They neither accepted nor welcomed their pure beauty. As if they couldn't believe what they were given was real. The sad destiny of all those beautiful hidden faces, all those walking masks!

How often we laughed about the new concept of bravery and courage in this age. As if it took an especially brave person to resist concealing, to resist masking.

I said, 'I'm confused whether you hate your red drinking face, or you're secretly in love with make-up. In both cases, you don't need to hide anything, you don't need to cover your face. I know and I can understand.' I wished I could say, 'We can understand', but the entire world had proved otherwise to you, way before I started my lessons as a child. I couldn't promise you anything on behalf of anyone else but myself.

I wiped the mad white away from your lips, eyebrows, nostrils, ears, forehead and shirt. I got you to drink some fresh water. You settled down. We looked deeply into each other's eyes. You searched mine, I searched yours. There was no barrier. It was all there: the unspeakable.

I was shattered by your unspeakable, you were grateful for finally having someone who truly understood. This is how our long gaze ended. We had no secrets. You were extremely exhausted. I put you in bed. You went to a deep sleep as soon as you hit the pillow. I set the alarm, so you wouldn't miss your first student who never in a million years could imagine what had happened that morning in the forbidden room. Indeed, silence holds unlimited possibilities, countless stories… it's just that I'm not sure whether we are fortunate not hearing it or unfortunate.

After you died, I couldn't have any drinks for two years. I would throw up before the holy liquid even reached my lips. It was as if I was throwing up for you, cleansing for you. I was vomiting all the helplessness and hopelessness I suffered all those years, for I couldn't help you, I couldn't save you. It felt like a curse. It made me even angrier because not only did you leave me but you were finally able to take away the pleasure of my vodka shots. As if it was a revenge for not having that one damn drink with you.

I mourned and mourned, day after day, month after month. But it wasn't your death that I mourned. I had grieved your death long before you actually died. I mourned your life. That excruciating bleak life…

Somehow, I was set free the day you left. The anxious wait was over. It finally happened. The torturous infinite countdown was over. It finally reached zero. It was time. I sensed zero with my entire being.

It was strange. I played that *Elegy* for hours, again and again, day after day. I couldn't breathe. I was drowning with all that pure oxygen around. I stopped breathing, then I threw out some air.

Sobbing was next, month after month, mourning your life. I sensed the way you left, head on the table, heavy swinging arms, two glasses, one to cleanse, one to forget. That paralysing suffocating wait was over. You could finally fly, I could finally breathe. That ominous desperate time.

I haven't touched the *Elegy* since that doleful year. I have consumed it right to the end; there's nothing left to play. As for my vodka, it has never tasted the same anyway, but I have learnt to enjoy it in a different way. I don't throw it up any more. It's as if I have discovered a new taste in it, a taste that takes me to a different path, a different journey. Who thought vodka could become a philosophical drink?

Anyway, happy birthday, although you were never happy about being born into this unfair madhouse. Guess what, the world has become even crazier than when you went for that very last drink. It is chaos. Innocent people are dead, are forced to leave their homes, their countries. The number of refugees and displaced people is more than that of World War II. It is the great exodus. Can you imagine? Who thought there could be a greater catastrophe than that fucking war?

I guess you could. You had a marvellous sense of what was going on in the world. That was partly why you suffered that much. You could foresee almost everything with that wonderful imagination of yours. You could see too much. You didn't look, you saw. You wanted to be deaf and blind, things that can't be possible for a musician. You were that sensitive and unique, because you could hear it all, see it all. Your strength became unbearable, became your worst enemy.

People couldn't catch up with you, the world couldn't catch up with you. You saw too much, remembered too much, felt too much. You were too present, too conscious, too awake, too aware...

You had it all, and others had none. I understand now. I've seen enough people from enough diverse backgrounds and professions to know that seldom do they remember, seldom do they see, seldom do they hear, seldom are they present.

The solitude was inevitable; you were always a couple of steps ahead of others. You were deeply tired of educating people to be sensitive, not sentimental. You were exhausted. You hated sentimentals. Bottom line, the world is more disgusting now.

You would hate it even more. Well, to be fair, you could have a great laugh at the entire Trump saga. That sarcastic laugh of yours! I can imagine all the jokes we could crack over Trump and the never-ending stupidity of the embarrassing human race.

I am glad there are still people out there to prove otherwise. The other day, I heard a war-zone journalist who preferred to focus on the fact that there are a lot more acts of kindness than criminal acts in these areas. He said that, despite the horrifying and inhumane situation in Afghanistan, there are many more stories about 'people helping one another to survive' than the brutal attacks of Taliban.

I admired his positivity and his attempt at seeing good out of evil, but why it has to come to this? I ask myself this everyday. It's as if nothing has changed since those two great wars. We still manage to have no shame. All these Europeans, settled here in Australia after World War II, have so many heart-wrenching stories. The best would be just having a five-week journey on a ship from places like Russia, Hungary, Slovakia and elsewhere.

But even these relatively safe and happy-ending stories are accompanied by such bitterness and longing for the home country that make you think how it could ever be wiped out from one's memory, one's soul, one's DNA perhaps.

I had M and L for lunch the other day. M's story was no different. How much I wanted you to see them. You could have, but you childishly decided not to. Remember, I played one of L's pieces in a concert; you hated it. I asked whether it was envy or hatred. You laughed and said, 'You know me too well.' After all, hatred is akin to love.

I told you many times L would understand. L is a marvellous man, not only for his sharp intellect and captivating imagination, or for his endless curiosity and pushing boundaries, or for his extreme generosity in passing down what he knows, or for his tireless efforts in educating free-minded musicians, or for keeping music alive in the Ghost City, but also for his vast wisdom. For he has embraced existence in its entirety; he glides gracefully through good and bad, simple and complex, pretty and ugly, light and heavy, sweet and bitter, Heaven and Hell. He too can see.

I was found again when my path crossed his. I tell him that I wish I could be like him. It seems he truly believes in the light at the end of the tunnel. He says by the time I get to his age, I will be. Hope… I say I doubt it. He says, 'You'll see.' But hope comes and goes. It seems it never grows roots. It's like gypsies; staying in one place never suits. I wish I could keep it in a safe for ever. I wish I could never let go of hope. But then, I hate anything encaged, even hope. If it has to rove, let it rove. If it has to roam, let it roam.

Anyway…back to M's story. Like many others, M and her parents left their war-torn country for a more hopeful start at the end of this planet. Well, we all know that so far, the northern side of the Earth hasn't been very promising. Hope this other end works its magic. Again, hope, hope! What is it with this hope and its uncanny business? No pressure, this-other-end! We hope.

M's family was meant to move to Argentina as M's dad's business partner had settled there during World War II and found it to be a liveable country. So the kids started learning Spanish, but only for a short time, as fate had something else in store for them.

A short while before leaving his homeland forever or, better to say, running away from what was once called home, quite by accident, on a street, M's dad met another friend whom he hadn't seen for a long time. They had a chat in a close-by café and the friend revealed that he and his family had a sponsorship through a friend who lived in Australia. However, the friend did not want to use the sponsorship and he offered it to M's dad, which he accepted after discussing it with his wife. Thus, Spanish lessons stopped, English ones started.

M's dad had his own share of horror in a concentration camp, but luckily they didn't keep him for long, as he had converted to Catholicism for a Catholic girl before the gloomy desperate times. So he could get away from it. Thank God he married that wonderful woman and converted for the sake of love. Otherwise, M would have had to grow up without a father.

The whole family embarked on a journey to the land of sun at this other end. M recalled how they had to hide all their money and jewellery in the heels of their shoes so no one could confiscate or steal their valuables.

Then I thought about my piano tuner, Pierre. He is French, a relatively new migrant. By new, I mean he came here about fifteen years ago. He tells me wonderful stories about his clients' pianos. Some are sad, some are happy. He found much silver and gold cutlery in old pianos he used to tune or restore in Germany and France. He even saw jewellery hidden there.

He says in Europe everyone knows what a dark truth lies behind this cutlery and jewellery. Pierre says it is almost impossible to trace who owned these pianos at the time of war, but on rare occasions current owners could find the descendants of World War II victims who once used to play on these antiques.

I cry as he speaks. These precious, exhausted pianos kept someone else's belongings for so many years after that ominous war in the hope of having their owners back. None returned. Heart-breaking stories.

Anyway, M told me about her mother and her high regard for Persian carpets and Persian wools and how the first valuable thing her mother bought in Sydney, when she could afford it, was a Persian carpet. They didn't even have a bed but they had to have a Persian carpet, because it was a sign of prosperity and belonging to a cultured class of society, something that was greatly missed in the new country, something that had lost its meaning, its value, in the host country.

It was as if her mother wanted to stubbornly preserve her identity. The never-ending quest of migrants/refugees who had to flee their home towns, and their ever-lasting longing for what they left behind! M still remembers that her mum got so mad when she heard an Aussie woman who called these beautiful carpets floor mats and complained about their expensive price.

To M's mum it was an unforgivable insult not knowing the difference between a precious work of art and a floor mat. Mum then sighed bitterly to show the cultural distance between herself as a refugee and a local.

All this happened in Sydney, back in the early 1950s, when M was only a little girl. M still remembers that day, in the only Persian carpet shop of Sydney. The memory of her mum's emotions and feelings are still very well alive.

M's story is not all about sorrows and the hardship of leaving everything behind. M mentioned humorously that who knows what would happen to L if we ended up in Argentina.

And there it is: a sudden glimpse of happiness and bliss, which looms in a dark history of war and escape. The absolute necessity of not losing the sense of humour, an essential requirement of survival!

L's dad had that sense of humour as well. L's family also had to leave their home behind. They were part of a Russian-Jewish community in China. After the horrible war, Mao ordered the foreigners including L's community to get out of China. Mao rightly said, enough is enough, you foreigners are the reason that we are so miserable and so addicted to opium. And the rest is history.

So L's parents decided to go to New York, where L's grandfather had already moved and Russian Jews were welcomed. In the US consulate, they realised that L and his brother could not get a visa because, unlike their parents, they weren't born in Russia. They were born in China, so they weren't counted as Russians.

The Americans only took about a hundred Chinese per year at the time, which meant L and his brother had to wait in a long queue to obtain a permit to enter the land of freedom and liberty. In response to how long they had to wait, L's dad was told about five years.

Back in those days, at the time of Mao and World War II, anything could happen in a second, let alone in five years. I wonder if anything has changed since then.

As L's dad walked out the consulate, he turned around and asked, 'In five years, is that in the morning or the afternoon?'

Thus reunion with Grandpa was not possible and they had to look for countries like Australia, which kept their doors open to increase their population.

Luckily, L's dad also had a friend living in Australia who recommended this other end of the world. Not so long ago, this other end was welcoming enough to embrace all refugees from different backgrounds. Nowadays, we have to protest against what this other end does to its refugees on Manus Island and in its other dungeons.

Anyway, M and L are among the lucky ones. There is no happy-ending for many other refugees. I still remember what Anna told me about her mother. She too had to run away from the catastrophe of post-war England. A highly educated woman who was trained as a pianist but was forced to study medicine to fulfil the requirement of being proper, as it was so improper for a woman to pursue a career in music.

Just like your mother. She too was first trained as a pianist but forced to study medicine in some university in Baku or Moscow. I can't remember where it was. That's how she met your father in the medical school. Unlike Anna's mum, she never finished her studies in medicine as she got married and brought up two kids who she forced to become musicians. Very ironic! I often wonder whether that was why she was so manipulatively controlling and dominating.

We could never forget about the demoniac role she played in your miseries. At least your dad was at ease with your secret. Being a physician, he knew it right from the beginning. To be fair, like Anna's, your mum was also a victim of her parents' decisions for her proper future. It's like a vicious cycle of having an unhappy and unfortunate life, generation after generation, which is imposed by parents who think they know it all.

Two sad women who had the same aspirations, living around the same time, but in two very different countries, in two very different cultures. Parallel lives of two repressed women! Women who could be brilliant if they were given the opportunity, women with heavy hearts who were forced to bury their dreams.

Imagine how our world would be different if they could have lived their dreams. Anna's mum's properness did not matter at all in World War II. It didn't matter that she was a doctor, or she belonged to a family of doctors. She never stopped wondering why she wasn't allowed to follow her dream just for the sake of properness and prejudice. I guess we can never understand why.

Anna's mum recalled that there was a great sense of solidarity and unity in England after the war. Everyone was stubbornly determined to build the ruins. Everyone helped one another, the same story as the war-zone journalist told about recent wars.

Anna's mum and her family eventually ran away to this other end; the solidarity was not enough to keep them in their home country. What they witnessed and experienced were beyond their tenacity, endurance and fortitude. They had to leave behind all the properness in London and never look back.

It seems Anna's mum could never let go of her ominous past. Anna always tells me that her mum hasn't aged well because she belongs to that generation of migrants. I hear these words while I'm looking at Anna's mum's mahogany upright piano, which is now in Anna's possession. Made in the early 1900s, with its gorgeous candle-holders and its quaint charm. It can't stay in tune for long but it has the most soul-penetrating mellow tone which constantly reminds me of a brilliant woman who heavy-heartedly carried the love of music, a doctor who couldn't go past the war, who couldn't treat her own scraped heart. She too drinks to forget.

That once-brilliant mind resides in a remote area in Victoria, deep in the bush, trying so hard to wipe her memory out. She might be dead by now. I don't know. I don't dare to ask. Of course, I never met her, for which I'm glad. That, I couldn't bear to see, knowing all her sufferings. I couldn't bear looking into her sad, lost eyes.

Anna's mum's cousin lived a better life, though. Another magnificent woman who could survive the bitterness of war against the odds. Her happiness didn't come easy and she had her own share of agony and being abused by a once-beloved husband.

Like Anna's mum, her husband couldn't bear what he witnessed during that destructive war. His fabulous London was never the same, despite all that sense of unity. Even the woman of his life was not enough. I hate these stories of defeated loves. He couldn't see beyond the ruins, he couldn't hear anything but the sound of explosions, shrieking children and moaning injured people. So he too decided to drink to keep himself blind, to keep himself deaf. Ten shots for not seeing, twelve shots for not hearing, every forty-four minutes, to the end of eternity. As there is no end to eternity, he was well assured that he could be infinitely blind, infinitely deaf.

Anyway, that was the prescription he followed. He truly shut down. He became a monster, sold his sensitive and fragile soul to Satan. I often wonder why he didn't sell it to Dionysus, who adored the intoxicating drink. He could have much more fun by doing so. I guess I will never know. He sold it in exchange for living a different life and wiping the memory of the past. I know, it's a bit Faustian.

He started hunting, torturing and then murdering the delicate soul of others who were once so precious to him, people whom he used to love dearly. And trust me, he did not spare anyone, even Anna's mum's cousin, whose love was the only thing that kept him going through the loathsome days of that fucking war.

Luckily, the cousin worked for *Vogue*, which demanded frequent trips to Germany. And indeed she took every chance to run away from the beast. Having said that, Beast left a black mark in the cousin's soul. He pushed her to follow his drinking rituals and God knows what other things he forced her to consume. But in one greyish autumnal afternoon the cousin's destiny changed drastically when her sad, lost, still eyes were staring out a window in an airport in Germany, pretending everything would be all right when she faced Beast at home.

Finally, a miracle happened to a miserable survivor of that fucking war. She was found again. Hope loomed out of the darkness. She was found by Yuri, a wealthy Russian business man who like many other Russian émigrés escaped the dream of social justice and preferred to be a gypsy and a world-wanderer with no homeland.

Yuri was mesmerised by the cousin's fragile figure and her sad blue eyes, which searched the void tirelessly. He was enchanted by her vulnerability, hidden with such mastery behind her pale motionless yet beautiful face. He couldn't take his eyes off her. To him, she was Ondine surfacing on the water, taking the last breath before disappearing in the deep, deep ocean.

Like you, Yuri could see. He didn't look. He saw and even sensed that woman from afar. Yes, he sensed every bit of that woman. Probably, Yuri was one step ahead of you because he had learnt how not to let go of what he loved and how to hold on to it tightly. Being a romantic man, he knew having her was a must. He knew he couldn't live a second without that lost Ondine. As he approached her, his chubby fingers let go of a cigar he was holding to make room for her hands. Thus the feverish passionate affair began.

They both had seen and suffered enough to know there was no time left to waste. They made love like there was no tomorrow, as if they wanted to compensate for all those who had lost their loved ones in that chaotic and agonising epoch. And indeed they did.

Of course, Ondine left Beast and started afresh. She never got lost again and lived happily ever after with Yuri in Germany, far, far away from the city of ghosts, the place which was once called home.

It's quite ironic that they both found solace in a country that caused their homelessness, a country that caused the greatest distress in the history of humanity. I know, I know, a country never causes pain, wretchedness, woe, and despair…people do.

Yuri could probably help you. He was a great music lover. You could speak Russian, so there was no barrier, at least language-wise. You could perhaps share your insight, your knowledge, your love of the Russian repertoire; he could perhaps teach you how to hold on to what you loved. I think Yuri knew the way or, better to say, found the way.

Sometimes, being a world-wanderer is the only way. But, of course, not everyone can be a world-wanderer, no matter how much one hopes. And, of course, not everyone is as lucky as Yuri.

Luck… Hope… Those two funny little things.

Take Ben's mum's luck, for example. Her story is heart-breaking. Unlike Anna's family, she wasn't an educated person, but she shared the same destiny. She belonged to an Italian working-class family who found refuge in this other end right after the unforgettable war.

If only Anna's mum's parents had known properness never matters in disastrous times. They burn every single one of us, proper or improper, educated or not.

Well, Ben's mum also couldn't have enough of any drinks. She got so busy indulging herself with the Water of Life that she forgot about a candle she had lit. The candle is now the symbol of her ecstasy. She too could never get over that fucking war.

Almost every single person I met from the older generation of refugees shares similar stories. Wars leave unforgettable pain, untreatable wounds. And we still cannot learn from the past.

About two years ago, a journalist found a wandering child with a plastic bag in the deserts of Syria or Iraq. I have a lousy memory. I can't remember where it was, but the footage was horrible to watch. It was spine-chilling like the worst nightmare you can possibly imagine, again very much like those abstract scenes of deserts by Dali. Yes, so bitter and terrifying it was, watching a lost child roaming all alone in a dessert, hanging on to a plastic bag in hope of finding a safe place, in hope of finding a familiar face, in hope of seeing his mum, his dad, once again. One could not stop crying seeing that surreal horrific footage.

All these years, I have been told that I play with a very sensitive touch. All these years, I responded with my brutal honesty, that it's all you, that I pass on your pain, desire, agony, love, anger and dreams. As if I have never owned that sensitivity.

Whether you like it or not, you live in me through my sensitive sound. I play my own sadness, desires and dreams too and I am not saying you were in charge of my finger technique. You were never interested in that. All of your students lacked the fine and polished technique. We were all these wild sentimentals who worked our arse off, and even raced off to be sensitives. Imagine if you could pass down your technique.

Why couldn't you care less about that? I still wonder. You knew very well that a sensitive touch without a refined technique doesn't get you anywhere. You were extremely generous in all other aspects but very strangely calculative and stingy about this. Does it mean you had lost hope way before we came to know it? Were we again years and years behind? It wasn't a fair-played game, if that was the case. You wasted our time in that regard.

Or, perhaps, it was your quiet revenge for the life you never had, revenge for all those torturing, fearful, anxious years of anguish. Your muted revenge for the slow, suffocating death of your colourful dreams, your brilliant golden touch...*perdendosi*...*smorzando*...*morendo*...for fading away, for dying away, bit by bit...sigh after sigh...a tormented soul...your silent subtle revenge...

Some of us, myself included, had a chance to further our studies. We worked on our wild undisciplined fingers, we learned to control those unleashed creatures. Teachers were amazed by our imagination, expressiveness and interpretation, but they were puzzled by our rough and not-so-refined technique as classically trained performers.

We were simply wild. You probably had a lot of fun imagining all those puzzled faces from Germany, Austria, France, America, England, Australia, Ukraine, and even Israel. Unfortunately, your game didn't reach China, Japan or Korea. So no puzzled faces over there.

I too am puzzled and confused to this day. Why didn't you pass down your knowledge? I would be lying if I said I don't care when people are thrilled by my sensitivity. At least I have done something right or, better to say, you did something right.

After all these years, I still wonder whether you really wanted to have a daughter or not. Or was the idea of a gay man having a child so out of reach in those days that you never allowed yourself to even think about it, even you, with that enviable imagination? Is that why you said I am not a daughter to you but a friend you never had? There are many things that I still wonder about you. You see, even soulmates can't fully read each other's mind.

Good news is that, nowadays, in some happier parts of the world, gay men and women can bring up loving daughters and sons with no fear, no shame. In some much happier places, they can even get married legally. I'm afraid this is the only good news I have for you. The rest of the world is dipping in a greater and deeper shit than when you went for that very last drink.

The Tree I Loved and the Mysterious Man

I was very philosophical today. Driving to work, passing along a road that once accommodated my beautiful tree, I was thinking about how much I always wanted to pull over on Cotter Road and sit on that magnificent branch. A branch that waited for me all these years to pull over. I never did. Never had time. And when I had time, I postponed my sitting on that old mighty thick branch. Because I wanted to have something to look forward to. Isn't it such a pathetic reason or excuse?

You know, Cotter Road is a very strange road. It's nothing like any other road. I always thought how lucky I am to live in a capital city that feels like countryside. Perhaps the only capital city that feels so close to nature. Magnificent ancient and not-so-ancient trees, horses, foxes, possums, rabbits, kangaroos, emus, rosellas, and countless other birds. Driving along Cotter Road, you always feel that you're under some spell.

At one end, you're led to this heavenly magical bushland that you can't stop exploring, you can't stop thinking about. You long to get back there. And then there's the other end, the end that bores you to death, mainly because you know heaven is at the other end and your life could be excitingly different if you could only be at that end.

Anyway, for some unknown reason, I finally managed to find something enchanting on the road to absolute boredom. The boredom lost its power the moment I spotted that curious stunning branch, the moment I was spellbound. That was the most inviting branch I have ever seen in my life. More inviting than those of wild cherries that I used to climb, more inviting than those of platanus trees, more inviting than those of any other trees. And trust me, I have seen many branches, climbed many trees. This was the one that always reached out to people, always generously offered its seat. As if it was made to have company.

Now it's all gone. All gone within *six* weeks, while I was having my summer break. Only six weeks, not sixty weeks, not sixty years, *six weeks*.

Got back to work on a Friday. Was shocked by not being able to see my tree, my branch. It was all gone, vanished, evaporated. The some-hundred years of history suddenly disappeared. Appalling!

We are funny creatures. Funny would be the polite way of describing our species. If we had a device that could translate the tree language into one of our own, we would never ever cut off these old trees. For they would suddenly become an invaluable treasure, a great source of information, shedding light on our past, shameful or honourable. I bet we would preserve them obsessively, we would water them, fertilise them, trim them, take the nasties away, we would even order special gems and jewels to embellish their lovely leaves and branches.

Every tree would be a Christmas tree. Not because we care about our environment or our history – so far we have made it clear none matters to us – but because trees, as the oldest residents of the earth, could reveal many secrets of this planet. Because trees have seen it all, heard it all, lived it all.

Trees with their travelling roots, reaching the unreachable, the dark abyss. Trees, treasurers of all hidden buried secrets. Dark lucrative secrets. Secrets like where you would be able to find more natural uranium for mass destruction. Trees, keepers of the night, guardians of the dark abyss.

I wonder why we have never been interested in secrets or mysteries other than dark ones.

For example, governments offer numerous PhD scholarships for research on war and its different aspects. There's nothing secret about it. Write an ordinary boring proposal, explain why war is going to benefit the human race, or the economic benefit of war, find a supervisor who shares your utopian ideas of war. Boom, you're in, money's yours, funding flows.

Just out of curiosity, I organised a coffee session with a PhD student who used one of these scholarships. I took nothing extraordinary from that conversation. Same old shit that we all knew before. Coffee was good, though, thanks to the masterful barista whose attention to detail transforms froths of his lattes into a spectacular work of art. He generously gives so much of his time to the froth.

The PhD student babbles, or better to say prattles. I just focus on the petals…a rose in my latte…thinking life is maybe the barista's careful attention to his roses, his love hearts, and his other abstract drawings that I can't figure out, life is maybe admiring his froth-embellishing techniques. I'm not hearing the PhD student any more, I'm drowned in roses, love hearts, trees, drowned in all the seconds spent by the barista to make his lattes inviting, welcoming, refreshing.

Maybe I have to close my eyes to the world, maybe life is immersing myself in roses, in petals, in love hearts. I guess I was hoping to hear something about the intricate diplomacy of wartime, something about saving more lives than losing, something about resolving conflicts, something more intelligent, something new, something cleverer, something different.

Deeper and deeper in love hearts, petals, roses, I forget the entire world. I know I am a silly useless naïve idealist. But imagine if governments could fund research on peace instead of war. If only we could imagine… All those poor old executed trees…

On the bright side, I'm glad we haven't yet invented the device to translate the tree language. If we did, we would have to start a business of tree-torturing in case there might be a tree reluctant to reveal the underground secrets of the earth. I'm saying *yet*, because I fear the day it happens. If it has to happen, I hope it's when I'm dead. If it has to happen, I hope it's in a billion years time.

Maybe I should delete the sentences about the device, in case there's a selfish lunatic out there who would do anything to make history by stealing the idea and inventing such a demoniac thing. After all, Jules Verne's fascinating stories are no longer imaginary. Quite scary!

On Cotter Road, where other trees were also gone, I thought to myself that I was away only six weeks, and see how my spellbinding world got destroyed. Could I have fought for those trees if I had not been away? Certainly could not. There were roadworks in progress. The ugly look of civil construction.

My gorgeous scenery, the one I yearn for. You know, I was very proud of noticing that branch. Today again the ugly site made me so nostalgic. What have they done to my seat? I was meant to pull over and experience sitting on it. Why did I think it would always be there, it would last forever? How childish! What the hell was I really thinking? That is still a mystery to me.

The funny thing is that I don't even know what the future plan is for this city, the city that housed scenic roads of which I was once very proud. And yet I thought the tree and its inviting branch would be immortal, would be eternal. I was so silly and stupid not pulling over because I was in a hurry. Or was I lazy? Or perhaps if I had pulled over I would have had nothing to look forward to on Friday mornings and afternoons going back and forth to work. I can't even remember what type of a tree it was. It wasn't a pine, it wasn't a willow. Maybe it was a strange-looking willow? Was it a gum tree? And it's not even two months since I saw it last.

It seems I'm no better than the others. I didn't see with my eyes wide opened. Pathetic. Maybe because I was always so mesmerised by the reaching-out branch that I never cared about the tree. Maybe! But there is no excuse; I simply didn't see. I looked but didn't see. I have a very clear vision of the setting, though: very green leaves with very green grasses underneath, with very thick and a slightly bendy branch.

Is my clear vision detailed enough? Pathetic. See, I didn't see. I always thought I could have some tea under its generous shade, sitting on its grand inviting branch. I thought about a hundred years ago and made up stories about people who could have had picnics there. I thought about seven hundred years ago when indigenous people could rest their backs against its trunk after a day of hunting, after returning from the other end where sacred rituals were performed among heavenly majestic rocks. Those peaceful days.

All my daydreamings are gone now. The road is not inviting, not exciting. Back to boredom. I wonder whether it's sad or actually fortunate that I never pulled over. Because if I had done so, I'd be even sadder today recalling a wonderful time I had with the branch, drinking my tea, watching rosellas, listening to rustling leaves, taking the sunshine in. Yes, maybe it was my good luck. I guess I'll never know.

Then I thought about many other things that I could have done but never did, countless moments that I missed. Was that good luck too, or had I simply missed my chances?

After all these thinkings, I went to the mall to run away from the soaring heat, which was reaching forty degrees. Right before entering the mall, I saw a young good-looking man, seemingly of my age. Was I hallucinating? After all, I don't do well in heat. I can severely dehydrate in a few seconds.

Maybe there is hope, maybe the tree is still there, maybe I'm so dehydrated, so dizzy that I can't spot my branch on that curious road.

He was familiar, though, looking at me with two ocean-blue eyes, with desires, with dreams. Not a sleazy look at all. Don't get me wrong. I couldn't be that dizzy. It was as if he was complimenting with his navy blues. There was something very honest and pure in his look. All this happened in a glance, less than five seconds.

I felt the weight of his look, I raised my head, looked into his gorgeous blue eyes. Well, I didn't know him. He had road-worker's clothes on. He could be a simple tradie, a sophisticated civil engineer, a philosophical architect or a wise plumber or a skilled carpenter or whatever. Or he could be the one who cut my branch, the one who brutally took my beloved tree out. What did they really do with my branch?

I had my sunglasses on. So I don't think he saw my eyes but he smiled at me. Maybe he had seen through my glasses, caught my suspicious eyes. His smile was pure, though, honest and simple, like his eyes. I thought I could be friends with him. He couldn't possibly be the one who executed my tree. Could he? Rushing fleeting thoughts, appearing, disappearing within five seconds. I couldn't get his look out of my head. The smile was stuck in my mind. After all, he looked very familiar, my stranger, mysterious admirer.

After an hour and a half hours of wandering in the shopping centre to save myself from melting, I finally remembered: he looked like our family friend's fiancé. I met him in our holiday house next to the dark blue ocean.

That day, I warned the bride-to-be that the guy carried some dark secrets, like those buried in the abyss. No one believed. It was there, right behind the eyes, his smeared lost soul. No one believed. They said I was a pessimist, they said I was a cynic with a bitter eye. But it was there, his smeared lost soul.

They said poor, poor shy fiancé. I said, 'God knows what's hidden behind that innocence.' That childlike face of his. He too had blue eyes. He couldn't hide behind his blue eyes for so long. The real self burst out soon, smudged everyone's lives. It was ugly, it was dreadful. It caused unbearable pain. Those countless unbearable days. If only they had dared to dig into those cunning murky blues. If only…

But he didn't bear my probing look for long. He couldn't even stand my presence. He avoided me for the rest of that historic day. It must have been so uncomfortable for him with all that probing and searching.

Poor, poor, shy fiancé with his monstrous side…master of domestic violence, master of cruel fights. He could beat like no other man. He even slapped the mother-in-law, in the court, in front of the judge. I still think about the way he bore all that anger under those cold silent blue eyes.

He was a child of a broken marriage. A boy who buried his sorrows, his frustrations, for so many suffocating years to feed his wild unleashed anger. There is no excuse for what he did, but I wish he had known there was help available before it was too late, before it was too dark. Those dim blue eyes…

I wish he were born into a different family, I wish he were born at a different time. I wish for many other things. I wish I had never seen through those demoniac brutal eyes...

The bitter memory ruins my admirer's complimenting gaze. Yes, the pleasure of that short tender moment did suddenly vanish. That slippery connection. But my mind was still challenged, for he had those two ocean-blue eyes, transparent, pure and bright.

I wonder why we would rather ignore obvious realities than face them. Why do we prefer to close our eyes to signs? Why do we have to learn our lessons through dramatic excruciating experiences, which could be simply avoided if we accepted the truth, if we saw the reality? Perhaps we're too busy to see. Or maybe too lazy?

Perhaps we're terribly scared of being alone. We'd rather risk our own life, our own soul, to avoid solitude. If so, what's the purpose of being soulless or lifeless? Or perhaps we're so scared of our own self that we can't be left alone by ourselves, that we prefer to be occupied by other dreadful experiences, by ignoring our true self. Then, when we have enough of it, we blame love. We say love is blind. Really? How blind can it be, I ask myself every day. We seldom say, 'I was blind.'

Take Jane, a post-doctoral fellow, well read (supposedly), well raised, well travelled, well everything. She too blames love for marrying her irresponsible husband, Bill.

They divorced many years ago, but they managed to add two unhappy daughters to their unhappy marriage, although they knew from the beginning, before they wed, that it wouldn't work out, that Bill was immature, that Bill was unreliable. As if Jane wanted to prove herself that Bill was Truly Immature, Truly Irresponsible.

I can't understand it at all. Doesn't this show Jane's own irresponsibility when she willingly decided to go with the immature unreliable package called Bill? Jane never says, 'I was blind.' It's either Bill or love that she holds responsible. It doesn't really go beyond that. She doesn't seem to be happy in her current relationship either.

Harsh as it might sound, I think Jane could reduce her unhappiness to a bearable extent only if she dared to admit to being sexually attracted to immature, irresponsible, lazy men.

Love didn't do any better for Jack and Jill either. They started a very passionate, feverish relationship in their twenties which made Jill, an urban girl, quit studying what she loved and pushed Jack, a farm boy, to settle in the city that he hated. Jill started studying something else; Jack pursued a lucrative career in the stock market. At least they were young and inexperienced when they madly fell in love.

Bill and Jane don't even have that excuse. They did all the wrong things in their mid-thirties, in the name of Love. Now they're hitting their fifties, they're still the same, nothing has changed. Damn Love.

It wasn't always bad for Jack and Jill, though. They shared many loving moments. It only went pear-shaped when the kids left home and they had nothing else to focus on but each other. It was time for them to face the reality of the life passed by.

Was it right for Jill to bury the idea of her dream job? Was it right for Jack to leave the farm life he always yearned for? Now the only commonality is the love of their children and the love of food. At least they still dine together and they don't famish in solitude. Nothing lacks in their lives money-wise. They have accomplished all their financial missions, dreams, desires. But their worlds are many miles apart.

There is something very Zen about Jill and the way she tries to tolerate Jack and his insipid jokes. As if she's on meditation for 24/7. As if tolerating Jack is a rite of passage leading to a spiritual blessedness. I won't be surprised if Jill becomes a hermit in a faraway secret temple in a lush, bushy, green, humid forest of Japan on an unmapped rocky mountaintop with impossible accessibility. But for now there is only a cold silent look between Jack and Jill after forty years of marriage. It freaks me out to see there's nothing left after a lifetime but the icy frost in their parched eyes.

You see, there is something sophisticated about Jill's attitude to life and living, something which is completely missing with Jack. He doesn't have the philosophical, poetic approach to life, as Jill does. Nor does he have the 'beauty in simplicity' factor. I can understand why. It's an extremely rare achievement.

Jill runs too. Jack teases these daily running rituals. He surely wouldn't if he could understand why. Jack boasts about his sheep-shearing skills, but even that is somehow uncomfortable to hear. It's incredibly hard to imagine Jack, with his posh existence, shearing sheep. I'm convinced that he was banished from the farm. There's something vicious about his sheep-shearing stories, something vampire-like. Maybe Jill runs to forget Jack's endless shearings, Jack shears to forget Jill's tireless runnings. Maybe!

All farmers I have seen so far have a unique, rather romantic, relationship with land, with nature, with living. I have seen a farmer whose massive library abounded with books on philosophy, poetry, literature, history of agriculture from the time of the Aryans in ancient Persia to the twenty-first century in the Netherlands, a farmer with the most poetic connection to his land, to his cows, to his trees, to a dilapidated cottage that housed three generations of aunties on that land. A farmer who felt connected to the rest of the world, who felt responsible for the well-being of all pastures, all trees, all animals, all seas, a pure global man.

With Jack, it's as if he sneaks into some random farms, uses his stock money to bribe an innocent farm boy to let him shear, to satisfy his shearing hunger. He craves shearing. I hope all these sheep-shearings happen under supervision. I truly fear for the safety of all sheep in the region. I can't stop thinking about the lamb roasts he serves at his monthly dinner parties. After all, he loves cooking, and we all know sheep after sheep he shears. Who knows, maybe shearing is a prelude to slaying, a prelude to sacrifice. I become an avid vegetarian each time I'm invited to one of Jack's roast parties.

And then there are his inappropriate jokes that are thrown at Elizabeth, who is all about politeness, properness and etiquette. Sitting at the table, I eventually burst into laughter, seeing the extreme contrast between the shearer and the romantic Elizabeth, goddess of femininity.

Of course, Jack thought I was amused by his jokes and presumably took pride in being a good host. Poor old Jack! An incredibly comic and hilarious scene…

I exchanged looks with dear Ellen, who shares the same sense of humour. But this time she was absolutely shocked by the extent of the awkwardness dominating the room. Her confused, puzzled face made me laugh even harder. Jack's face shone with pride, assuming he was the funniest man alive. I could barely stop. I was possessed. As if the laughter had a separate entity, a distinct uncontrollable existence. As if it was sitting next to us, forcing me to laugh mischievously, forcing Jack to levitate in euphoria, in a state of sheer contentedness, forcing Elizabeth to practise tolerance while appalled, forcing the atheist Ellen to thank God that she didn't marry a man like Jack.

That powerful, demonic laughter! Poor Elizabeth is in her early eighties and reminds me of my grandma whom I miss extremely since she died a few years back. The resemblance is mind-blowingly unbelievable. The light rose-pink skin, the facial structure, the sharp wide-open honey-green eyes, the dainty physique, the intense interest in David Attenborough's wildlife series, the love for the piano, the sense of curiosity, the shy laughter, the hand that covers the mouth when laughing, not because of poor oral hygiene, but because sometime in their distant youth they were told that it was 'unladylike' to laugh aloud, to reveal teeth perhaps. I have even checked or, better to say, examined from afar Elizabeth's ears. Strikingly unbelievable.

Elizabeth's home is as neat as my granny's. She too embroiders everything: handkerchiefs, placemats, tablecloths, pillowcases, skirts, dresses, you name it. Trust me, these types of ladies can embroider wood, rock and even steel. These types are all about making and creating, nothing escapes their skilful fingers. The dexterity of creative hands.

This is the universe talking to me in its own way. My grandma is incarnated. I bet Elizabeth crochets too. It's almost impossible to embroider without crocheting. I don't know why, but it seems crocheting and embroidering go hand in hand, a match made in heaven. I bet a dancelike gesture of the arm or the hand tempts Elizabeth to pick her nose too. I bet Elizabeth's philosophical nose-picking was caught, at least once, by her granddaughter. Only granddaughters are capable of lurking behind walls and prying into their grandmas' affairs.

I bet there is a small floral patterned jug of fresh lemonade in Elizabeth's fridge waiting for her granddaughter. I don't exaggerate when I say both Elizabeth and my granny look like Agatha Christie's Miss Marple. All three are annoyingly observant. All three dress the same, wear their hair the same.

Maybe this is not the universe but Agatha who is talking to me from the ruins of Egypt, from the pyramids. Maybe this is Marple incarnated twice, once as my grandma, once as Elizabeth. Maybe…

I bet Elizabeth makes shawls and tea cosies for her granddaughter. My tastefully crocheted white shawl is an eye-catching phenomenon. There is something enigmatic, something spellbinding, something captivating about it, something that you can't ignore. As if it permeates life, permeates being, permeates pure existence. Nothing has made me prouder than this marvellous shawl.

I took it to the world, to the farthest ends of the earth, from the farthest south to the farthest north, from the east to the west. No one has gone past unnoticed. My unmissable grandma, living in the shawl. My travelling white magic. Adults, teenagers, men, women, all those chasing gazes. Bold ones simply ask where I bought the delight; shy ones confirm the magic with their admiring eyes. Even kids can't pass by without asking.

Just the other day, my seven-year-old piano student reached out to touch the irresistible delicate magic. He was enchanted. He is the curious mind, doesn't practise much, but is all ears, all eyes. He feels the vibration under his tiny fingers. He longs to see the hammers, the strings, the damper, week after week, lesson after lesson, he asks to see. He is amazed every time. I wouldn't be surprised if he invents a new model of piano in twenty years' time.

The sound fascinates him. Mozart, Beethoven, Dvořák fascinate him. Stories fascinate him. He thinks German-speaking parents have a strange taste. I ask how come. He says, 'I know they're good at music, but who would name his kid Gang of Wolf, Wig of Lud?' I burst into laughter. He's still hanging on to the white magic.

I think to myself, my granny adored kids.

He says mischievously, 'Gang of Wolf played for the king when he was six. I can't even play for our prime minister.'

I assure him nothing is impossible; he just has to practise. I have to assure him dreams come true otherwise why bother dreaming, right? His colourful dreams.

He can't resist the irresistible any more. 'Did you buy your scarf in Sydney?' He doesn't know it's called a shawl.

I ask why Sydney.

He says, 'Sydney has the most elegant fancy stuff.'

I'm surprised he knows the word elegant. He knows the meaning too. He feels the shawl with such delicacy.

I say, 'No, my grandma made it.'

He merely says, 'Wow!' A simple humble wow with sharp greenish eyes, carrying all the wonders of the world.

He then invites me to the Lego exhibition. He says, 'Today we play the piano, tomorrow we play Lego. It'll be great fun.' He has planned it all.

I hate to disappoint him but I would be in the magical bushland, among the sacred rocks, at the heavenly end of the road.

He says, 'Who leaves Lego for bushwalking?'

I say, 'You're right. I'm a bit crazy.'

He keeps trying. 'We'll be there for the whole day, in case you want to join after bushwalking.' He sighs. 'I wanted to show your scarf to my mum.'

My captivating shawl…

Then there is my ninety-year-old-plus class, the zealous inspiring bunch whose tenacity inspires me every week. They're all about trying and trying…ageless minds, ageless hearts. Their eyes sparkle with every new note, every new sound. They notice the shawl right away, even the ninety-three-year-old Ada with her dim eyes. I photocopy everything in A3 for her. She is into the business of knitting. She knits and knits, with yellows and greens. The dexterity of creative hands.

She touches my shawl. She says with envious eyes, 'I was never good at crocheting.'

I wonder how she sees. She uses her third eye; she feels the magic love.

She says, 'I've memorised the theme, so I don't have to look at the sheet.' She plays and sings, 'AAC#-FDD-DDCBb-GGG-GAGFE-DC#Bb.' Her hands shine. Invincible fingers, decorated with golden rings, eight rings for eight precious fingers, thumbs are spared…eight embellished playing fingers…those shiny hands, covered with Vaseline, saving the tired brittle skin.

She wants to learn to the end. A solemn rite, sitting in her room, getting ready for her weekly lessons, starting with her shy faint pink lipstick, brushing her dyed curly hair, preparing her magic fingers, first with her shy pale pink nail polish, then the ointment; finger after finger she ornaments.

She looks at me, those marvellous beaming eyes. She hopes she got it right this time, she hopes it was better than the previous week, she hopes she hasn't disappointed me. A wrong note here and there. Does it matter at all? A tone higher or lower. Does it disturb the vast universe? I ask myself every time she plays. Isn't it all about the journey, the time she spent on rewriting her melody in letters, with her tired eyes, those that brighten up every time she learns a new theme? Isn't it all about the time she spent on adding her left hand, for she believes in use-it-or-lose-it. Isn't it all about her love for music, the love she had to leave behind, for there was no money? A tone higher or lower, who am I to disturb her love, her dream…

I think of my friends, those who have stopped touching the whites, touching the blacks, those who have sold the magic box, for they couldn't bear to look at the forbidden love, the unachievable dream, those who won't even play for fun. I wish they knew it was not about a wrong note here and there, a semitone higher or lower. I wish they kept playing those heavenly sounds. I wish they had never lost their trust in their magic fingers. I wish they had never succumbed to dreamless teachers who forgot it was all about love, teachers who managed to steal dreams of countless artistic minds. Those resentful bitter souls, envying youth, envying imagination, envying crisp fresh ideas, envying hope, envying the dexterity of young creative fingers… Those who shattered music.

The irony is that these witless teachers were not true musical talents dominating concert scenes in Carnegie Hall or Albert Hall, or any other hall. True talents use their endless gift to encourage students, to encourage the love of music, to promote acceptance, to promote tolerance. True talents found West-Eastern Divan Orchestra, true talents make music in hope of a better understanding of humankind. True talents give. True talents try. True talents are not into crushing dreams.

I wish my friends knew their journey mattered, their voice mattered, their playing mattered. All these burnt dreams. A wrong note here and there, a semitone higher or lower. I ask myself every day.

I tell Ada that I think it was perfect. Am I wrong? A beautiful smile, refreshing a gorgeous little face. Lustrous eyes. She wants to learn a new piece. Who am I to disturb her dreams?

Ada believes I understand her tireless knittings. Scarf after scarf, she shows me her yellows and greens. No one asks whether my granny is dead or alive. Maybe they don't dare hear the bitter truth, especially after they are so moved by its unique charm. Perhaps it doesn't matter at all, for the shawl is so alive, so magnetic, so hypnotic. Perhaps the shawl is my granny, perhaps everyone could see but me. No wonder I feel warmer whenever it's around me…her warm hugging hands… No wonder my tea tastes better whenever I use her crocheted tea cosies… that delicate elegant touch.

She lives in those Liszts, Mozarts, Brahms and Bachs we used to watch together. Liszt's consolations, Liszt's études, Liszt's concertos. Watching and watching, Liszt after Liszt, tea after tea. So far away are my Lisztian days with my astonishing granny.

I wish I could freeze time, that moment she looked at me with those sharp honey-greenish eyes to declare her love for Liszt's music. I wish I could freeze time, that moment I said she would be one of those helpless romantic fans fainting at Liszt's concerts if she were living at his time. I wish I could freeze time, that moment she giggled and never denied. Those escaping moments, those distant days…the days she was mesmerised by Gulda's artistry, amazed at his ability to conduct and perform that fascinating piano concerto, that mesmerising Mozart…. AAC#-EDDDDCBb-AGG-GAGFE-DC#Bb…

Seemingly unimportant moments, lasting in your mind for a lifetime. Fleeting faces, running past my eyes…Jack, Jill, Jane, Bill, Ellen, Elizabeth, Grandma, Ada, Gulda, Liszt, Agatha, Marple, Fiancé, the admiring ocean blues, the ephemeral tree… Short-lived, passing, delicate, fragile contacts…

Fleeting immortal moments. Or perhaps fugitive visions, escaping to the endless void, shaping me, shaping you…

Matures

Well, if you must know, I'm sitting at a round table, facing the window, looking at the trees, seeing recently blossomed flowers. Yes, I'm in my town house in Canberra, at the end of some winter in some year.

Hi, friend! Take in all the fresh air, inhale the sweet smell of blossoms, try to memorise the smell, the colour, the shape, for they don't last long, for they soon disappear and what you'll be left with is the memory of how they looked, how they smelled, how they smiled.

Thinking about my past, present and future. Wasn't this always my job? Thinking and thinking, pondering and pondering, past, present, future, past, present, future, round and round? Outcome: all these years of thinking have made me an expert thinker. Ha! Ha! Ha! Funny, hey?

Having said that, you should add the habit of dreaming to that of thinking. Outcome: an actual lunatic. Why a lunatic? Well, I don't find myself like that but most of the time I come to this understanding that they consider me as a harmless lunatic, a harmless dreamer, a harmless local eccentric.

'Can't you see, *woman*? these things can never ever happen.' Or even in a much harsher way: 'When do you want to grow up? Stop fantasising about things!' As if their maturity has helped them improve their sad pathetic lives, as if their 'maturity' has created a better world. Jesus, I wonder why they don't mind their own business. I wonder why they want to drag you down to their barren realm of maturity.

What is happening there that I'm missing? I ask myself everyday. How are they different? Better what? Nicer what? Better humanity? I doubt it. Look at all these wars and displaced people. It's chaos. Better understanding? More wisdom? I doubt it again. Deeper knowledge of being? You tell me about it.

Well, I'm saturated with Matures' positive thoughts that are sent on my way. I've heard them millions and millions of times, and perhaps when you finish reading these reflections, I mean my reflections or, better to say, my deliriums, or whatever you like to call them, you would add another million to my millions and millions of times.

What can we do with all these positive vibes around us? Run to the mountains? Be a recluse, leaving the fantastic barren world to Matures? I don't know, but I do run to mountains over and over, using nature to toughen up, reminding myself that I have to be like wild stubborn tulips, forcing my way out of hard rocks, searching sun, searching light, welcoming bees, welcoming flies. Those invincible wild tulips.

I do think and think, read and read, dream and dream, play and play, and then I do it all over again, but backwards, play and play, dream and dream, read and read, think and think. Why? I'm not sure, but somehow this system suits me best. I think we need to order a new pair of eyes, though. Or, better to say, a new set of eyes. Maybe we have to order two sets, in case we lose one.

It's quite obvious that the way we have been reading so far hasn't been helpful or useful at all. I'm convinced it's our eyes' fault. We simply need new fresh eyes. That's all. Eyes that truly read, truly think, truly dream. Yes, they can think. Haven't you heard of thinking eyes? Eyes are everything. After all, they are the window to our soul, demonic or angelic.

Anyway… Let's be clear now. I won't be a recluse. That would make it too easy for Matures. I mean, they can't get rid of me so easily. Matures don't realise they are the reason that I am what I am. Matures, creators of this chaotic time. Perhaps the timing of my birth was not right. I shouldn't have been born at this time, or the past time for that matter. I don't see much difference between the present and the past. Both are confused anyway.

Whether I like it or not, I was born into this confused time, like the way people are born into a wealthy or poor family, cultured or uncultured, educated or uneducated. I was born into this chaotic time.

I'm a child of revolution child of war child of peace child of many rights and wrongs child of fear child of hope child of executions child of births child of environmental concerns child of global warming child of technology child of carnality child of spirituality child of communism child of capitalism child of esotericism child of rationalism child of junk foods child of culinary delights child of wealth child of poverty child of… Yes, I'm a child of this Dickensian time.

Remember the opening of *A Tale of Two Cities*? Nothing has changed. It's a funny world. Anyway, Matures have figured it all out. It's heaven in Matures' time zone.

'You silly dreamerrrrrrr!' Matures say, while glaring at me, thinking I'm wasting the air they breathe.

I think we all need to work hard on our imagination. It sucks at the moment. We can't even imagine a life with no war, no hatred, no viciousness, no illness. We're so busy planning and rehearsing our survival strategies.

I'm not sure why Matures hate my dreamings so much. Isn't it a fabulous thing to imagine a wiser, greener, compassionate, peaceful world, to go beyond rights and wrongs? Oh! I know, I'm asking too much. I've always asked too much. Matures are so religiously busy administering and safeguarding their precious maturity. Their intense focus reminds you of something like the medieval concept of virginity and the sacred act of protecting it. In other words, Maturity, nowadays, is equivalent to virginity in Dark Ages. No surprise there; we sure know that History repeats itself in a different guise. I hope there is no surprise. It has always been like that, even before the Dickensian time. I wish History were fed up with this lame cycle, so it could stop regurgitating the same old shit. Oops! For a second, I forgot that Matures are in charge of History. Never mind, regurgitation it is.

I'm personally thankful that they're creative enough to change its guise every time History needs to be repeated. At least they can imagine to that extent. Imagine if the Chernobyl accident had to happen every time in Ukraine. That would be a disaster. Thanks to Matures – and

God, of course – this type of 'accident' can happen anywhere these days.

We're so unbelievably lucky that they've given it good thoughts. Anyway, it would be good if we could be open to everything and everyone. Just open, nothing more.

But Matures are freaked out by the idea of being open. Matures don't have time for this; they're way past this stage. Remember, Matures are busy making History. I wonder why the world is a big mess now. Oh! I know why. There's History and its unmistakable mistakes. Well, it's extremely hilarious that Matures always hold History responsible. It's always History's fault that we make the same mistake over and over. 'How on earth History could make that horrible horrible mistake again? Silly, silly old History!' Matures say. History and its unfathomable role in our miseries. History's silly mistakes, ruining every aspect of individuals' lives. Aren't Matures the funniest creatures of all time? So cute and adorable.

Anyway… All I have truly learnt until now, in my short life, is how good it feels when you dream and how it sucks when a day goes by with no dreaming. As simple as that. Quite childish, quite naïve. Quite a cliché, but I wish you could feel good as well. There's nothing sophisticated or complicated about this. You would think anyone could understand, even a Mature. Well, you have no idea. You would probably say, 'Is that all you've learnt through your thinking and thinking, reading and reading?'

I would answer, 'Well, yes and no at the same time. I have learnt about other things too, but I won't discuss it with you for free any more. I'm afraid it costs you a lot more than you expected. The price for you, my friend, is being exposed to all ideas from different parts of the world. But I'm not sure if you can afford it.'

Some probably could, but I have to sell it to them like that, because once they're told that they cannot afford something they do whatever they can to own that poor thing; they would use all their power, all their contacts, all their inheritance; they will do anything. Trust me, they will spend countless dollars to show off what they can afford. Same old story, we never change, I'm afraid it's not rocket science to anticipate our moves, our reactions, our behaviours, I'm afraid we are not as intricate or as intelligent as we were promised.

Even our wars are like that. Someone says to someone, 'You can't have our oil, our natural resources, our land' or 'You can't afford to pay the right price for our oil or our natural resources', then the one who receives the bad news about the impossibility of possessing someone else's natural resources, land and life does everything in his/her power to achieve the unachievable, to attain the unattainable.

Result: centuries and centuries of conflict and catastrophes for the human race, Matures and Immatures. Imagine if Trump was told that he could not afford peace or he could not have peace. He would stomp his grotesque calloused fat feet like a spoiled brat and he would make sure that he had peace the next day. Isn't it pathetic that we're viciously eager to own what we can't have and easily let go of whatever we have?

Let's talk about money. The stupid money is what we're all concerned with: our mature politicians, priests, clerics, our mature university lecturers, teachers, physicians, musicians, poets, writers, philosophers, environmentalists, conservationists, our every mature professional.

I'm not kidding. Take one of our very mature supervisors, supervising by the tick tock of the clock, because time is money, because mature supervisors are not paid enough to spend enough time with students, because there is no funding, because they're too busy producing journal articles every couple of months to secure their suffocated existence in a place which once housed those who were interested in knowledge only, housed those timeless people. I don't think there are many timeless people left in the world, thanks to Matures again.

Soon it will be a time of huge scarcity, trust me. Poor supervisors, they can only guide you to an extent these days. You wonder whether they're forced, or even threatened, to be supervisors; you wonder whether they are dishonest in their expression of interest; you wonder whether they know anything at all, whether funding is an excuse, whether they too had supervisors who were only worried about money, calculating the 'probability' of their survival in what was previously called the House of Knowledge before the invasion of Matures, before money was this enormous issue. You pity them, for they seem so miserable, so much in need of those few dollars, that you prefer to be a lone seeker, finding answers by yourself, not bothering those poor destitute supervisors, not even removing them from your panel, because you fear for their financial future, for the impact that little money has on their mature lives. After all, they tell you that they receive little money.

And then if they come across a unique, priceless supervisor who is not into the business of moneymaking, they would say that he/she is lucky to be able to work for the sake of knowledge, that he/she is lucky to be even successful. Lucky to be alive perhaps, as their bitter jealous eyes bulge out with envy.

Mature supervisors never blame themselves for the current situation; they pretend they too are the innocent victims of the system. They can't see that we're all the creators of the fucking system; or perhaps they see, but they're better off keeping their eyes tightly closed, their mouths tightly shut. After all, it took them years to penetrate the House of Knowledge, wipe those timeless people out.

Now it's Matures' time… Matures' revolution… The reign of Matures… It seems Matures can be as destructive as termites when the enticing scent of money permeates the air. Their behaviour around money reminds you of some pagan rituals with dancing naked bodies, stoned and intoxicated, around a bonfire. The transcendental power of money.

Don't get me wrong. Matures have taught me well. They have made me understand that money is the answer to everything we seek. Thanks to Matures' constant reminder, there hasn't been a day that I haven't been thinking about money. If only I had money, if only I'd won that lottery, I would have built the House of Knowledge, once again, from scratch, safeguarded it from Matures, filled it with timeless people, those that money can't buy, priceless people…brilliant minds who are all about knowing, learning, seeking, giving – yes, those priceless people with massive hearts, with broad visions, with generosity of no kind.

Sadly, I still need money to rebuild the House of Knowledge and emancipate it from Matures. Well, it would be better to win that damn lottery soon. I wonder whether we'll soon be like Russians or Chinese who bribe their lecturers and supervisors to get a proper education. I won't be surprised if in twenty years' time there's no kid who knows the answer to 3x3, because there'll be no money for that, because governments can only fund up to 3x2 and teachers can only afford up to 3x1.

I don't think I have to wait that long, though. It's quite shocking at the moment anyway. Based on Matures' own calculations, about forty-four per cent of our adult population lack literacy skills required for everyday life, let alone numeracy.

Maybe I'm aiming high. Maybe the fund would only cover up to 2x10. Ah! Matures, Matures. You see, it's quite frustrating. It seems nothing helps – thinking, reading, dreaming, all useless.

And then there are our mature musicians. Take Alan, a chubby brass player in his fifties, with messy hair, and glasses so dirty that you wonder how he sees. Well, maybe it's out of genius that he never bothers to clean those glasses. After all, a blurry world is nowadays better than a transparent one.

Unlike other Matures, Alan doesn't need to close his eyes to not see. He simply doesn't clean his glasses. A more convenient way to blindness. See, he's ingenious, he's all about short cuts, saving time. He can already see what he wishes to see. And, of course, he uses his creative mind to visualise what could be behind the haze. There are mounds and mounds of money behind that haze. He's already on a very good salary, thanks to his own maturity and the generosity of other Matures who couldn't see him wasting his magnificent talent in immature orchestras.

You see, there is a mutual understanding between Matures of every profession. Matures sense each other. When the Mature scent pervades the air! You don't want to know how it smells. I'm afraid it stinks like a six-week-old sweat. That's how Matures find each other.

Anyway, Alan is on a job-hunt these days. What he has now is not enough. Not that he's musically talented; it was never about music anyway. He goes city to city on his break from that mediocre mature orchestra, bragging about his current hundred-grand salary package, complaining about the boring canonic repertoire he has to play every season. But Alan never plays in tune, because he's terribly bored of the canonic repertoire; he doesn't practise either. No wonder nothing tuneful comes out of the poor brass. Maybe that's why he complains.

I knew Matures were blind but had no idea they were deaf too. Alan proves his species lacks two major senses. Now I'm feeling sorry for the Mature cohort. It's truly not their fault then. They can't see and they can't hear. I wonder what else they're not able to. Now I'm glad they have their own orchestra, untuned instruments for a bunch of deaf audiences, a match made in heaven. After all, their concerts are another spiritual ritual to meditate on their dollar-chasing abilities. The deafening experience is truly mystical.

Now, Alan is ready to commence his next stage of spirituality or, better to say, spiritual maturity. Finally, ruining all those Beethovens, Mozarts, Haydns earned him a promotion he worked his arse off for. He's ready to leave the nest, ready to ruin Brahms, Schumann, Tchaikovsky and, if he's lucky, Mahler. I'm afraid he's still three levels away from killing Stravinsky, Rachmaninoff, Prokofiev. But you know, he is Alan, he always aims high. He never fails to mention that a job he seeks has to pay way more than a hundred grand.

I'm convinced he has his eye on Stravinsky, Rachmaninoff and Prokofiev, on the third level. Otherwise, he wouldn't insist on the amount of money he's after. He's a well-informed Mature, knowing the market, knowing the price. Alan's mature taste is very sophisticated, though. He's bored with murdering Beethoven, Mozart and the like, and, at the same time, he can't get himself to listen to Stravinsky, Rachmaninoff, Bartók, Berg and Prokofiev. In fact, he can't stand twentieth century music at all. He says, 'It's the music for the madhouse.'

I wonder which madhouse he's talking about? The one Matures are in charge of? Yet he's happy to play this awful repertoire as long as he's paid more than a hundred grand annually. Not that he plays well or in tune, remember?

Of course, we should never ever forget that he is already on the hundred grand and he won't waste his precious intellect on anything less than that amount. Alan's world is complex. He hasn't yet expressed his sophisticated opinions about twenty-first century composers. I should perhaps thank all existing and non-existing gods for that.

Despite his maturity, he doesn't get that twentieth century music, like any other music, reflects its time, reflects those horrible wars, reflects the chaos, reflects all those dead people, reflects the darkness, reflects the anger, the dread, the grief, the loss, the pain, reflects hope. You would have thought that he had understood it by now, after all those Beethovens, Mozarts, Haydns. But, no, he hasn't got it. Or maybe he has. He's just playing the game of denial, a game popular among Matures.

Or maybe, like those termity mature supervisors who invaded the House of Knowledge, Alan is on a mission to sneak into the unreachable orchestras and gnaw them away. None of the twentieth century composers escapes his eagle eye; he is like an encyclopaedia, he can order them alphabetically, and then hate them alphabetically, from Adler to Boulez, Scriabin to Strauss, Ravel to Xenakis, he hates from A to Z. As if he's running a hate campaign of some sort.

I think the fact that Alan can't stand the music of these people is a credit to all composers who wrote anything in the twentieth century, from the first second of 1900 to the last second of 1999, composers who made it difficult, uncomfortable and even impossible for Matures to enjoy their ritualistic concerts with this music. There is no doubt that this music has challenged Alan to his core. He knows very well that this repertoire costs him a lot more than the game of denial.

I can't stop laughing imagining Alan's choked, intimidated face in Mahler's symphonies, or Stravinsky's *Petrushka*, or the *Rite of Spring*. Poor Alan. Deep down, Alan knows that even five hundred grand a year is not worth risking his blood pressure, mental health and nervous system. After all, this is the music for the madhouse, right?

So, for now, this repertoire is safe from the gnawing Alan, but I wish he could stop wearing that annoying T-shirt. I promise, I will leave him alone the moment he does. That ridiculous T-shirt he always wears; trust me, always….

It's a light blue one with a print of the Statue of Liberty with the *No War* motto. You wonder how many of these T-shirts he has bought. You hope he washes it regularly if he has only one.

Anyway, I'm not sure why he's interested in this particular print when he denies the bleak aftermath of the horrible events of the twentieth century, when he still fails to understand what happened not so long ago. Current wars don't bother him either. It seems he has no clue about the scale of catastrophe cursing the entire twentieth century, cursing five continents, war after war. He denies the scale, the impact.

Maybe he's from a different planet. Maybe he's a robot, programmed to ignore anything unpleasant, to deny anything savage, anything brutal. I can't believe how he thinks, what he says. It's pretty bad, even by Matures' standards. Even a Mature keeps up appearances. I wish he were joking.

Sometimes I think he's a rare brainwashed Mature of Nazi descent. So you wonder what he likes about the T-shirt that he wears every day. Is he camouflaging? Is he a dressed-up robot? Is he being ironic, sarcastic? Is it the colour he likes? Is it the statue he fancies? Is it the optimism promised by the statue? Is it the word, war? Is it no war? Which war is he thinking of? The war between Matures and Immatures, perhaps? Is it the idea of liberty? What is it that he wants to liberate, to set free? Well, with a hundred grand, he can certainly afford another T-shirt.

Maybe it's simpler than I think. Maybe someone has complimented the T-shirt and now he can't take it off. Or maybe it's just another costume for the role he plays in his daily affairs, in his job-hunts, the role of a nagging brass player who uses a T-shirt to make a good impression, because it conveys a message that he knows will sell well in today's world. Yes, he's dangerously clever and diplomatic.

He knows very well that even an understanding, like-minded Mature would not employ him if he revealed his true beliefs in the job interview. After all, it's all about keeping up appearances. So he stays quiet and lets the T-shirt do the job for him; no words are exchanged. The T-shirt itself speaks aloud.

I've always feared Alan-like people. He knows the Statue will stand tall whenever he steps inside a room to hand in his résumé, the one which boasts his effortless ability to ruin compositions of timeless people. He knows the Statue will stand tall whenever he picks up the poor brass to kill Mozart, Haydn, Beethoven. He knows the Statue is a good disguise.

Mature Mature Alan, a diplomatic dangerous walking mask. I know, I know, by now half of the mature population is having heart attacks and the other half is blowing into paper bags to calm their panic attacks. Jesus, time for your Second Coming, perhaps?

Love and Death

Love

This is for you, my dearest friend. Remember you asked me whether your passionate love for your beloved would cause you pain, would leave you, once again, with a broken heart? Well, I'm finally ready to answer, but have some strawberries first; they always help you feel better.

Love is everything. Isn't it? Love is vast, love is diverse. Love is everywhere. Isn't it? Love is family, love is friend. Love is pet, love is plant. Love is passion, love is lust. Love is darkness, love is light. Love is now, making the moment; love is then, recalling the time gone by. Love is life, love is death. Love is nostalgia. Love is melancholia. Love is hysteria. Love is personal, love is abstract, love is subjective. Love is happiness, love is bliss. Love is smile, love is scowl. Love is laughter, love is sob. Love is calm, love is furious. Love is shiver, love is fever. Love is trying, love is stopping. Love is loss, love is hope. Love is forgiving, love is forgetting. Love is doubt, love is dream. Love is blind, love is wise. Love is pure, love is murky. Love is desire, love is fear. Love is peace, love is war. Love is simple, love is complex. Love is music, love is sound. Love is fondness, love is kindness. Love is hatred, love is love. Love is revenge. Love is numb. Love is yearning, love is longing. Love is languishing, love is flourishing. Love is all, love is none.

I'm not sure why you always ask me questions that I can never answer. Is there any answer to your question at all? Are you pulling my leg again? I wonder. You always dared to love again and again without knowing. Whereas for me, I dared love once. That was amazing, don't get me wrong, but also dreadful and exhausting at the same time. I'm sure it shouldn't feel like that!

We crave being loved, but we hesitate to love. I wonder whether the human body is designed for that at all. That's probably why lovers barely remember love, like the rest of the population. Maybe love is lost. But when did it get lost? Has it long been lost?

Did love exist at the time of ancient Greece, at the time of ancient Persia, at the time of the Mayas, at the time of the Incas? Did it get lost in the medieval tortures, in the countless brutal invasions that History has reported so far? I have no idea. Maybe after all, the human body is not designed for love.

Anyway, I found my love in the high mountains, in the crimson of dawn, crimson of dusk, in the pristine white of snow, in the shimmering of ice, where you suddenly come close to your pure self, where you become one with rocks, one with tulips, one with snakes, one with eagles, one with thunder, one with clouds, in mountains where you embrace the entire nature, where you unexpectedly face your fears, face your beauties, face your unknown dreams and desires, face your true self, in mountains where you are one step closer to understanding your existence as a human being, where you are finally nature.

I'm trying hard to remember how I felt on that day, that moment, that second. My memory sucks. I can't even remember my historic love, the only time I dared love. Quite embarrassing after all I've said so far.

One thing I'm clear about, though. It was a day that I decided to love like Christian Bobin's characters. Remember how his characters could actually become pregnant by being in the state of love? Remember, one of the women could fly up high in the sky every time she fell in love, as if she were one of Chagall's paintings, the one with the floating woman, roaming above the city, the weightless woman in the air. She was light, gently propelling, gently hovering, like a feather, like a bubble. That blissful lightness…

I was that woman that day in that moment, inflated, impregnated, light, weightless, floating on the clouds, floating on the rocks. The more inflated, the higher I went, the more I saw, the lighter I became.

All I can remember is that I couldn't stop floating. It was so addictive, so exciting. I flew and flew, higher and higher, floated above all pointy mountaintops. I could have gone further up, I could have surpassed Mount Everest, if only I had kept floating. I wish I could stay in those mountains, gliding over trees, flying above peaks. If only I had kept floating. If only I had never landed on this gloomy gritty ground. How I long for that featherlike lightness!

You know what? I'm not to blame. But I wish I knew they would gaze with suspicious eyes. I wish I had never left that mountain. I wish I knew they wouldn't believe in love. I wish I had kept floating away and away, higher and higher, further and further.

On the bright side, I think it's definitely time to disturb the world with our love. It's long overdue. Wasn't it Eliot who asked, 'Do I dare disturb the universe?' I think daring and disturbing it is. Wasn't it Sohrab Sepehri, the Persian poet, who said, 'Eyes are there for gazing, wet with the tears of *loving*.'*

I think we have kept our eyes blind long enough. I think our eyes have long dried out. Our poor suspicious eyes, these glass eyes. If only we dared.

In the meantime, have some strawberries. At least they refresh your tired love.

Death

You hear about a dear friend. You say you knew it, that you felt it, that you sensed it. You shut down. You sob. You cry. You play. It has to be Beethoven. It has to be *Appassionata*. It has to be the third movement. Your fingers madly move. You drink. It has to be water, just pure, pure water. You play and play, sob and sob, cry and cry. You drink that cold, cold water. You stop. You are mute. You are cold. You become the silence. You go for a run. Your heart races. It gets colder and colder,

---

* I am grateful to Yeganeh Atri and Paul Flottman for their careful translation of Sepehri's verse.

your heart flutters. It feels heavy, it feels numb, it feels empty. It is dark. It is cold. It is pain. It is anger. Sheer solitude. Your eyes ache. Your toes ache. Your throat sobs. Your heart is wrung out, it is crushed. Pain scrapes the heart. You can't breathe. You try and try.

You play again. It has to be *Ballade*. It has to be Chopin. It has to be the G minor. You play the void. You play the silence. You play the grief. You play the solitude. Your mad, mad fingers. You fight the truth, relentlessly, heavy-heartedly, cold-handedly. It is bitter, it is cruel. It is despair. It is woe.

Once you were bright, once you were light. Now you count the countless hollow spots. You fear tomorrow, you fear the coming moment, you fear the excruciating pain, you fear the mournfulness, you fear the loneliness. You play and play, again and again…empty-handedly…

It has to be Brahms, it has to be the *Intermezzo*. It has to be the A minor. Mad tired fingers… You are the silence, you are the loss, you are the cold, you are the dark. You are that frosted roving soul. You are that frozen wandering ghost. You are that futile cycle of loving and losing, loving and losing, loving and losing…

Fragments

Have I told you that I saw my old self again, the one I used to catch up with every day, every minute? The old self, although short-lived, was worth looking at. You know, it's quite rare to find my self. When I do, though, I can't have enough of it. It's hard to leave home the days it appears. I keep looking and looking, then I have to let go and leave the mirror. Then I rush back to it, for I fear I will lose my old self in a second. I look and look, then I leave the mirror again. No puffy face, no puffy cheeks, no swollen nose. I'm amazed how I once looked. I'm amazed how quickly I forgot.

After a couple of minutes, I get back to the mirror, checking whether the self has disappeared or not. I'm relieved; it's still there, hasn't left yet.

I fear the swollen days. I look at my lips, my nose, my cheeks, my chin, my eyebrows, my eyes, the tame serene look. Yes, I look at my look, no swollen gaze. I try to memorise every detail for when I lose my self again…my ears, my forehead, my hair, my eyes, again and again. I am saving it for tomorrow, for the coming moment, for the second I am not able to find that self. One more trip to the mirror. Ah! What a relief! Quite narcissistic, I know. But I have to memorise it.

Is it narcissistic? But it can vanish in a blink. It's like smoke, once you are so sure, so certain that you have entrapped your old self, it smokes away. It slips. It fades away. It evaporates, so quickly, so rapidly that it makes you wonder whether what you saw in the mirror a few seconds ago was actually real, makes you wonder whether you have found your self at all at that short escaping moment. It melts away.

I dread the swollen days. Rushing back to the mirror. Anxious!

*

Have I told you that I feel so far away sometimes that I am so far away sometimes? Not in the past, not in the future. I'm right here, in the present, but so very far away, kind of in a still time, or as if time stops and I move further and further away from where I stand, but yet in the present, or as if I'm afloat above Now.

That sense of stillness, that static feel of time, far away in the sheer Now. It's hard to explain; it's almost like playing a piece. Sometimes the piece takes you to the past, sometimes to the future. Sometimes you're just frozen, frosted in Now, the present, far away with the music.

It's like Angela Hewitt's philosophical touch when she plays those enchanting Bachs, when she searches the space between every single note, when she fills corners of every single sound…when she adds, with her profound deep thoughts, you are the sheer Now, but far far away.

It's like Roy Howat's silky dreamy tone when he plays Debussy, when he treasures poetry in that short humble Schumann…when he adds, with his profound deep thoughts, you are the sheer Now, but far far away.

It's like Larry Sitsky's melancholic rubatos when he plays Rubinstein, when he hovers gently above the keys, drifting you away with care, when he mesmerises beyond nostalgia…when he adds, with his profound deep thoughts, you are the sheer Now, but far far away.

It's like Michael Kieran Harvey's bold honest imagination when he plays Sitsky, when he seeks light in *Dimensions of Night*, when he finds answers roaming through ancient Gods…when he adds, with his profound deep thoughts, you are the sheer Now, but far far away.

I'm glad sound never dies.

*

Have I told you I'm so dead and so alive? It's a strange state of existence. I have never felt like this before. It's hard to explain. It undoes my beliefs, undoes my views, undoes whatever I have learnt to date. Teases knowingness. It makes me rewrite, relearn, replay my life, everyday from scratch. It's a curious state. So dead, so alive, I tell two friends. One thinks it's poetic, the other is Silence at its infinite end. Fire and ash, day after day…

*

Have I told you identity is a very fragile thing? A very white Australian tries to beat a very patriotic Belgian, counting the years of Australia's white cultural history, counting the years of Belgium's independence. Every hour counts, every day counts; year after year he adds, 1788, 1830, 1839… A Canadian who doesn't compete, who thinks there's no chance, confused with her white dates, simply forgets those countless days of magnificent Indian history.

A very white Australian, a very patriotic Belgian, a very disheartened Canadian all defeated, counting the years of Persia's ancient past. A very silent Persian. Identity is a fragile thing. The very calculative historian forgets he was born and bred in a land boasting 60,000 years of magic wisdom, if only he knew victory was his, not the Persian's. He is busy calculating the white years.

The very homesick Belgian forgets she belongs to many more years of European civilisation, forgets that all Europe is her family, forgets Austrians married the French, the French married the English, the English married the Spanish, the Spanish married Italians, Italians married Germans, Germans married Russians. Russians married Turks, Turks married Hungarians, Hungarians married… She forgets she is not only a Belgian.

The silent Persian thought if only they were all gypsies, belonging to everywhere, or perhaps nowhere. If only they all heard about the latest verdict, the one that said we were one old family, carrying the black blood, teasing the white history, a big African tribe.

A silent Persian-Australian, a disheartened Canadian-Australian, a patriotic Belgian-Australian, a white British-Australian all in the borrowed land, the longest ride to the ancient Aboriginal site, the sacred rock...

*

Have I told you there is only a thin glass between me and a rosella that is eagerly eating my feijoa fruits, that is determined to strip my tree? He picks one and drops one, he picks one and drops one. He doesn't get bored with all these pickings and droppings. Maybe he's so hungry, maybe he's playing, maybe the fruit is heavy for his tiny claws. Or maybe he's just clumsy.

I can easily distract him, easily disturb him, easily scare him. But I'm enchanted by this futile exercise of picking and dropping. Maybe picking and dropping means something sublime in the rosella world, maybe it's an act of transformation, an act of transfiguration. Maybe! One can only wonder. A rosella with a persistence unknown to humankind.

I do nothing. I stay still, looking through the thin glass, waiting for him to give up. He picks one, drops one, waiting, picking, dropping, waiting, picking, dropping...

*

Today, I made friends with a filthy fat fly. I normally resent flies or, to put it more aggressively, I hate flies. But today, when I was sitting in the backyard, forcing breakfast bites down my throat, sobbing madly, a fly suddenly understood me.

You know, I never have my brekkie outside. But today I couldn't even breathe inside. A strange feeling of suffocation thrust me outside. It was more like throwing me up. You know that awful disgusting taste in your mouth when you vomit? It felt like that. The inside vomited me out to the backyard. For some strange reason, outside felt less suffocating. I had to eat something, but there was that soury, tarty, salty repugnant taste of vomit. It's been two days since I had anything worth calling food. That pukey smell.

And there it was, my understanding, filthy, fat, fly. He flew a couple of times around me and my food, then he just sat still on the balustrade. We looked at each other for a long time, I with my two swollen eyes, he with his five creepy ones. We both shared red eyes.

Who thought the filthiest creature of all time could be the only living thing in the world that could not only sense, but also understand my fucking inconsolable existence? Today, a filthy fat fly offered me, very generously I must say, an understanding that none of the humans around me was capable of. A cohort of sterile, uninspiring humans versus one filthy fat fly! No need to say who the winner was. Of course, the fly, in case you can't guess, and I don't want any misunderstanding regarding this matter.

He had no interest in my food. He kept rubbing his hands as flies do, but unlike other flies, his hand-rubbing rituals seemed more like an invitation to a hug than cleaning his dirty, scummy hands. Yes, it felt as if he wanted to give me a hug, as if he sensed my anger, my sorrows, my regrets, my frustrations. Yes, he sensed it all with those creepy compound eyes. I could never ever think, not even in my wildest dreams, that I would come to wish that I could hug back an understanding, remarkable filthy, fat fly. There we go again! Nothing is indeed impossible.

Who thought a disgusting fly could soothe my unspeakable pains? Who thought I would philosophise over this revolting creature that I hated throughout my entire life. Lesson learnt. Then I thought, 'Since I can't hug him back, I better offer all my food.' Time to reciprocate his truly munificent generosity with my humble offerings.

But, of course, he had no interest in my food. We kept looking at each other, I with my two swollen eyes, he with his five creepy mysterious yet familiar ones. I think we have met before. It feels like that anyway.

Oh! Now, I know. It's not his large dark-reddish eyes that are creepy. They're merely reflecting the world he sees. Those wise compound eyes!

I always knew we needed more than two eyes to make sense of our earthy world. If only he could lend me his precious wise eyes. God knows how many compound eyes we need to comprehend our world, let alone the universe. No wonder there are countless telescopes on the earth, facing the cosmos, registering every noticeable astral move. If only I could borrow all the creepy wise eyes of his entire clan! The fatter the clan, the bigger the eyes. And I need it all. My filthy, newly befriended, fat, flying friend…if only you knew how much you made my day today!

www.ingramcontent.com/pod-product-compliance
Lightning Source LLC
Chambersburg PA
CBHW030916080526
44589CB00010B/332